ROYAL COURT

Royal Court Theatre presents

MY NAME IS RACHEL CORRIE

The writings of Rachel Corrie
Edited by **Alan Rickman** and **Katharine Viner**
Produced with the kind permission of Rachel Corrie's family

First performance at the Royal Court Jerwood Theatre Upstairs,
Sloane Square, London on 7 April 2005.

MY NAME IS RACHEL CORRIE

The writings of Rachel Corrie
Edited by **Alan Rickman** and **Katharine Viner**

Cast
Megan Dodds

Director **Alan Rickman**
Designer **Hildegard Bechtler**
Lighting Designer **Johanna Town**
Sound and Video Designer **Emma Laxton**
Associate Director **Tiffany Watt-Smith**
Production Manager **Sue Bird**
Stage Managers **Charlotte Padgham, Katherine West**
Costume Supervisors **Iona Kenrick, Jackie Orton**
Set built by **Miraculous Engineering**
Set painted by **Charlotte Gainey**

THE COMPANY

Hildegard Bechtler (designer)
For the Royal Court: Forty Winks, The Sweetest
Swing in Baseball, Blood, Terrorism, Blasted, The
Changing Room.
Other theatre includes: By the Bog of Cats
(Wyndham's); The Goat or Who is Sylvia?
(Almeida); The Master Builder (Albery); Iphigenia at
Aulis, The Merchant of Venice, Richard II, King Lear
(RNT); La Maison de Poupée (Theatre de l'Europe,
Paris); Footfalls (Garrick); The St. Pancras Project
(LIFT); Electra (RSC/Riverside/Bobigny, Paris);
Hedda Gabler (Abbey, Dublin/Playhouse, London);
Coriolanus (Salzburg Festival).
Opera includes: War and Peace, Boris Gudonov,
Peter Grimes, Lohengrin, The Bacchae (ENO); Lady
Macbeth of Mtsensk (Sydney Opera House); Paul
Bunyan (ROH); Les Dialogues des Carmelites
(Japan/Paris Opera): Simon Boccanegra, Peter
Grimes (Staatsoper, Munich); Don Carlos, Wozzeck,
Katya Kabanova (Opera North); Don Giovanni
(Glyndebourne); La Wally (Bregenz
Festival/Amsterdam Musik Theatre); and most
recently the acclaimed Ring Cycle (Scottish
Opera/Edinburgh Festival).
Film and television includes: The Merchant of
Venice, Richard II, The Wasteland, Hedda Gabler,
Coming Up Roses, Business as Usual.

Megan Dodds
Theatre includes: Up for Grabs (Wyndham's);
As You Like It (Williamstown Theatre Festival);
Hamlet (Young Vic); Popcorn (West End); Smash!
(Intiman Theatre); English Made Simple (Primary
Stages); School for Scandal (Broadway); The Illusion,
Four Dogs and a Bone (Berkshire Theatre Festival);
Ashes, All's Well That Ends Well, Undiscovered
Country (Juilliard).
Television includes: Malice Aforethought,
Grammercy Park, Poirot, Spooks, Sword of Honour,
Love in a Cold Climate, The Rat Pack.
Film includes: Festival, Purpose, Bait, Interstate 84,
Urbania, Ever After.

Emma Laxton (sound and video designer)
For the Royal Court: The Weather, Bear Hug, Bone,
Food Chain, Terrorism.
Other theatre includes: Break Away (Finborough),
The Unthinkable (Sheffield Crucible); My Dad is a
Birdman (Young Vic), Party Time/One For The Road
(BAC); As You Like It, Romeo and Juliet (Regent's
Park Open Air Theatre).
Head of Sound at Regent's Park Open Air Theatre
in 2001 and 2002.
Emma is Sound Deputy at the Royal Court.

Alan Rickman (director)
Theatre: The Winter Guest (Almeida/West
Yorkshire Playhouse); Wax Acts (Gielgud).
Film: The Winter Guest.
As an actor for the Royal Court: The Seagull, The
Grass Widow, The Lucky Chance.

Johanna Town (lighting designer)
For the Royal Court includes: A Girl in a Car with
a Man, Food Chain, Under the Whaleback,
Terrorism, Plasticine, Fucking Games, I Just Stopped
By To See The Man, Mr Kolpert, The Kitchen, Ashes
and Sand and Where Do We Live, Shopping &
Fucking (with Out of Joint/West End); The Steward
of Christendom (with Out of Joint/Broadway).
Other theatre includes: Guantanamo Bay (Tricycle
Theatre/West End/New York); Macbeth (Out of
Joint); Someone Who'll Watch Over Me
(Northampton Theatre Royal); Via Dolorosa (Out
of Joint/Broadway); How Love is Spelt (Bush);
Permanent Way, She Stoops to Conquer, A Laughing
Matter (Out Of Joint/RNT); I.D. (Almeida Theatre
& BBC 3); Badnuff, Mr Nobody (Soho); A Doll's
House (Southwark); Six Degrees of Separation,
Ghosts, Misfits, Richard II (Royal Exchange); The
Dumb Waiter (Oxford Playhouse); Brassed Off
(Liverpool Playhouse/Birmingham Rep); Popcorn,
Les Liaisons Dangereuses, Playboy of the Western
World (Liverpool Playhouse); Feelgood, Little
Malcolm & His Struggle Against the Eunuchs
(Hampstead/West End); Rose (RNT/Broadway); Top
Girls (West End) and Arabian Nights, Our Lady of
Sligo (New York).
Johanna has been Head of Lighting at the Royal
Court since 1990.

Katharine Viner (co-editor)
Katharine Viner has been editor of the Guardian's
Weekend Magazine since 1998. She has twice been
named Newspaper Magazine Editor of the year.

Tiffany Watt-Smith (associate director)
As assistant director for the Royal Court: Almost
Nothing, At the Table, Blood.
As a director, theatre includes: Kismet, Mud,
Venezula, Trash, Teatro X La Identidad (Arcola);
Misterio Buffo (NT Studio); Honour (Young Vic
Studio).
Awards include: Jerwood Directors Award at the
Young Vic 2004.
Tiffany is International Associate at the Royal
Court.

THE ENGLISH STAGE COMPANY AT THE ROYAL COURT

The English Stage Company at the Royal Court opened in 1956 as a subsidised theatre producing new British plays, international plays and some classical revivals.

The first artistic director George Devine aimed to create a writers' theatre, 'a place where the dramatist is acknowledged as the fundamental creative force in the theatre and where the play is more important than the actors, the director, the designer'. The urgent need was to find a contemporary style in which the play, the acting, direction and design are all combined. He believed that 'the battle will be a long one to continue to create the right conditions for writers to work in'.

Devine aimed to discover hard-hitting, uncompromising writers whose plays are stimulating, provocative and exciting'. The Royal Court production of John Osborne's Look Back in Anger in May 1956 is now seen as the decisive starting point of modern British drama and the policy created a new generation of British playwrights. The first wave included John Osborne, Arnold Wesker, John Arden, Ann Jellicoe, N F Simpson and Edward Bond. Early seasons included new international plays by Bertolt Brecht, Eugène Ionesco, Samuel Beckett, Jean-Paul Sartre and Marguerite Duras.

The theatre started with the 400-seat proscenium arch Theatre Downstairs, and in 1969 opened a second theatre, the 60-seat studio Theatre Upstairs. Some productions transfer to the West End, such as Terry Johnson's Hitchcock Blonde, Caryl Churchill's Far Away and Conor McPherson's The Weir. Recent touring productions include Sarah Kane's 4.48 Psychosis (US tour) and Ché Walker's Flesh Wound (Galway Arts Festival). The Royal Court also co-produces plays which have transferred to the West End or toured internationally, such as Conor McPherson's Shining City (with Gate Theatre, Dublin), Sebastian Barry's The Steward of Christendom and Mark Ravenhill's Shopping and Fucking (with Out of Joint), Martin McDonagh's The Beauty Queen Of Leenane (with Druid), Ayub Khan Din's East is East (with Tamasha).

Since 1994 the Royal Court's artistic policy has again been vigorously directed to finding and producing a new generation of playwrights. The writers include Joe Penhall, Rebecca Prichard, Michael Wynne, Nick Grosso, Judy Upton, Meredith Oakes, Sarah Kane, Anthony Neilson, Judith Johnson, James Stock, Jez Butterworth, Marina Carr, Phyllis Nagy, Simon Block, Martin McDonagh, Mark Ravenhill, Ayub Khan Din, Tamantha Hammerschlag, Jess Walters, Ché Walker, Conor McPherson, Simon Stephens, Richard Bean, Roy Williams, Gary Mitchell, Mick Mahoney, Rebecca Gilman, Christopher Shinn, Kia Corthron, David Gieselmann, Marius von Mayenburg, David Eldridge, Leo Butler, Zinnie Harris, Grae Cleugh, Roland Schimmelpfennig, Chloe Moss, DeObia Oparei, Enda Walsh, Vassily Sigarev, the Presnyakov Brothers, Marcos Barbosa, Lucy Prebble, John Donnelly, Clare Pollard, Robin French, Elyzabeth Gregory Wilder and Rob Evans. This expanded programme of new plays has been made possible through the support of A.S.K. Theater Projects and the Skirball Foundation, The Jerwood Charity, the American Friends of the Royal Court Theatre and (in 1994/5 and 1999) in association with the National Theatre Studio.

In recent years there have been record-breaking productions at the box office, with capacity houses for Joe Penhall's Dumb Show, Conor McPherson's Shining City, Roy Williams' Fallout and Terry Johnson's Hitchcock Blonde.

The refurbished theatre in Sloane Square opened in February 2000, with a policy still inspired by the first artistic director George Devine. The Royal Court is an international theatre for new plays and new playwrights, and the work shapes contemporary drama in Britain and overseas.

INTERNATIONAL PLAYWRIGHTS

Since 1992 the Royal Court Theatre has placed a renewed emphasis on the development of international work and a creative dialogue now exists with theatre practitioners all over the world including Brazil, Cuba, France, Germany, India, Mexico, Palestine, Russia and Spain. All of these development projects are supported by the British Council and the Genesis Foundation.

The Royal Court has produced new International plays through this programme since 1997. Recent work includes At the Table and Almost Nothing by Marcos Barbosa, Push Up by Roland Schimmelpfennig, Ladybird by Vassily Sigarev and Terrorism by the Presnyakov Brothers.

My Name is Rachel Corrie is produced by the Royal Court International Department:

Associate Director **Elyse Dodgson**
International Administrator **Chris James**
International Associate **Tiffany Watt-Smith**

PROGRAMME SUPPORTERS

The Royal Court (English Stage Company Ltd) receives its principal funding from Arts Council England, London. It is also supported financially by a wide range of private companies, charitable and public bodies, and earns the remainder of its income from the box office and its own trading activities.

The Genesis Foundation supports International Playwrights and Young Writers' Festival.

The Jerwood Charity supports new plays by new playwrights through the Jerwood New Playwrights series. The Skirball Foundation funds a Playwrights' Programme at the theatre. The Artistic Director's Chair is supported by a lead grant from The Peter Jay Sharp Foundation, contributing to the activities of the Artistic Director's office. Bloomberg Mondays, the Royal Court's reduced price ticket scheme, is supported by Bloomberg. Over the past eight years the BBC has supported the Gerald Chapman Fund for directors.

ROYAL COURT
SLOANE SQUARE

Jerwood Theatre Downstairs

12 May–18 June 7.30pm
THE WOMAN BEFORE
by **Roland Schimmelpfennig**
Translated by **David Tushingham**

Directed by **Richard Wilson**
Design: **Mark Thompson**
Lighting: **Johanna Town**
Sound: **Ian Dickinson**

Sponsored by **Coutts & Co**

Jerwood Theatre Upstairs

6–28 May 7.45pm
INCOMPLETE AND RANDOM ACTS OF KINDNESS
by **David Eldridge**

Directed by **Sean Holmes**
Design: **Anthony Lamble**
Lighting: **Paul Anderson**
Sound: **Ian Dickinson**

Supported by
JERWOOD NEW PLAYWRIGHTS

BOX OFFICE
020 7565 5000
BOOK ONLINE
www.royalcourttheatre.com

AWARDS FOR
ROYAL COURT

Jez Butterworth won the 1995 George Devine Award, the Writers' Guild New Writer of the Year Award, the Evening Standard Award for Most Promising Playwright and the Olivier Award for Best Comedy for Mojo.

The Royal Court was the overall winner of the 1995 Prudential Award for the Arts for creativity, excellence, innovation and accessibility. The Royal Court Theatre Upstairs won the 1995 Peter Brook Empty Space Award for innovation and excellence in theatre.

Michael Wynne won the 1996 Meyer-Whitworth Award for The Knocky. Martin McDonagh won the 1996 George Devine Award, the 1996 Writers' Guild Best Fringe Play Award, the 1996 Critics' Circle Award and the 1996 Evening Standard Award for Most Promising Playwright for The Beauty Queen of Leenane. Marina Carr won the 19th Susan Smith Blackburn Prize (1996/7) for Portia Coughlan. Conor McPherson won the 1997 George Devine Award, the 1997 Critics' Circle Award and the 1997 Evening Standard Award for Most Promising Playwright for The Weir. Ayub Khan Din won the 1997 Writers' Guild Awards for Best West End Play and New Writer of the Year and the 1996 John Whiting Award for East is East (co-production with Tamasha).

Martin McDonagh's The Beauty Queen of Leenane (co-production with Druid Theatre Company) won four 1998 Tony Awards including Garry Hynes for Best Director. Eugene Ionesco's The Chairs (co-production with Theatre de Complicite) was nominated for six Tony awards. David Hare won the 1998 Time Out Live Award for Outstanding Achievement and six awards in New York including the Drama League, Drama Desk and New York Critics Circle Award for Via Dolorosa. Sarah Kane won the 1998 Arts Foundation Fellowship in Playwriting. Rebecca Prichard won the 1998 Critics' Circle Award for Most Promising Playwright for Yard Gal (co-production with Clean Break).

Conor McPherson won the 1999 Olivier Award for Best New Play for The Weir. The Royal Court won the 1999 ITI Award for Excellence in International Theatre. Sarah Kane's Cleansed was judged Best Foreign Language Play in 1999 by Theater Heute in Germany. Gary Mitchell won the 1999 Pearson Best Play Award for Trust. Rebecca Gilman was joint winner of the 1999 George Devine Award and won the 1999 Evening Standard Award for Most Promising Playwright for The Glory of Living.

In 1999, the Royal Court won the European theatre prize New Theatrical Realities, presented at Taormina Arte in Sicily, for its efforts in recent years in discovering and producing the work of young British dramatists.

Roy Williams and Gary Mitchell were joint winners of the George Devine Award 2000 for Most Promising Playwright for Lift Off and The Force of Change respectively. At the Barclays Theatre Awards 2000 presented by the TMA, Richard Wilson won the Best Director Award for David Gieselmann's Mr Kolpert and Jeremy Herbert won the Best Designer Award for Sarah Kane's 4.48 Psychosis. Gary Mitchell won the Evening Standard's Charles Wintour Award 2000 for Most Promising Playwright for The Force of Change. Stephen Jeffreys' I Just Stopped by to See the Man won an AT&T: On Stage Award 2000.

David Eldridge's Under the Blue Sky won the Time Out Live Award 2001 for Best New Play in the West End. Leo Butler won the George Devine Award 2001 for Most Promising Playwright for Redundant. Roy Williams won the Evening Standard's Charles Wintour Award 2001 for Most Promising Playwright for Clubland. Grae Cleugh won the 2001 Olivier Award for Most Promising Playwright for Fucking Games. Richard Bean was joint winner of the George Devine Award 2002 for Most Promising Playwright for Under the Whaleback. Caryl Churchill won the 2002 Evening Standard Award for Best New Play for A Number. Vassily Sigarev won the 2002 Evening Standard Charles Wintour Award for Most Promising Playwright for Plasticine. Ian MacNeil won the 2002 Evening Standard Award for Best Design for A Number and Plasticine. Peter Gill won the 2002 Critics' Circle Award for Best New Play for The York Realist (English Touring Theatre). Ché Walker won the 2003 George Devine Award for Most Promising Playwright for Flesh Wound. Lucy Prebble won the 2003 Critics' Circle Award and the 2004 George Devine Award for Most Promising Playwright, and the TMA Theatre Award 2004 for Best New Play for The Sugar Syndrome. Linda Bassett won the 2004 TMA Theatre Award for Best Actress (for Leo Butler's Lucky Dog).

ROYAL COURT BOOKSHOP

The Royal Court bookshop offers a range of contemporary plays and publications on the theory and practice of modern drama. The staff specialise in assisting with the selection of audition monologues and scenes.
Royal Court playtexts from past and present productions cost £2.
The Bookshop is situated in the downstairs ROYAL COURT BAR AND FOOD.
Monday–Friday 3–10pm, Saturday 2.30–10pm
For information tel: 020 7565 5024
or email: bookshop@royalcourttheatre.com

MY NAME IS RACHEL CORRIE

Rachel Corrie

was born in Olympia, Washington, USA, on April 10th, 1979.

Before completing her studies at The Evergreen State College in Olympia she joined other foreign nationals working for the International Solidarity Movement in Gaza on January 25th, 2003.

This text has been edited from her journals and e-mails.

Olympia, Washington. A bedroom. Clothes, books everywhere.
RACHEL *lies on top of it all.*

Every morning I wake up in my red bedroom that seemed like
genius when I painted it, but looks more and more like carnage
these days. I blink for a minute. I get ready to write down some
dreams or a page in my diary or draw some very important
maps. And then the ceiling tries to devour me.

I wriggle around under my comforter trying to find a ball
point, a Crayola, anything fast. I can hear the ceiling spit and
gnash above me. Waiting for me to look, because if I look, it
can eat me.

And I struggle for some socks and some boxers so I can make
a run for it – but I haven't done laundry in a month and the
other girl who lives in my room when I'm not here – the bad
one who tends the garden of dirty cups and throws all the
clothes around and tips over the ashtrays – the bad other girl
hid all my pens while I was sleeping.

And I try. I try to look at my fingers. I try to look at the floor
with all the fashion magazines left by the bad other girl, to find
one pen – just one pen. But I can't imagine where any pens
might be, and trying to imagine, I get off guard for a minute
and my eyes roll up towards the sky and I'm fucked now – I'm
fucked – 'cause there is no sky. There's that ceiling up there
and it has me now – 'cause I'm looking at it and it's going to
rip me to pieces.

She sits and faces us.

I am a creator of intricately decorated bedrooms. Each time
I move, I spend weeks painting, gluing things to my walls,
choosing the precise pictures of goddesses and art postcards.
This is a labour of love, and I become completely immersed
in it.

I wonder why I didn't notice the awfulness of my room before.
I am inside a terrifying mirror.

I glued things to the wall. My God, I glued things to my wall.

Touching the pictures, picking up books.

The question is always where to start the story. That's the first question. Trying to find a beginning, trying to impose order on the great psychotic fast-forward merry-go-round, and trying to impose order is the first step toward ending up in a park somewhere, painted blue, singing 'Row, row, row your boat' to an audience of saggy-lipped junkies and business people munching oat-bran muffins.

And that's how this story ends, good buddy, so if you are concerned with the logic and sequence of things and the crescendo of suspense up to a good shocker of an ending, you best be getting back to your video game and your amassing wealth. Leave the meaningless details to the poets and the photographers.

And they're all meaningless details, my friend.

She finds a journal and turns the pages.

1991.

My name is Rachel Corrie. I am twelve years old. I was born on April 10th, 1979 in Olympia, Washington, to my mother and father, Craig and Cindy Corrie, a brother, Chris, a sister, Sarah, and a really old cat named Phoebe.

I grew. I learned to spell cat, to read little books. When I was five I discovered boys, which made my life a little more difficult. Just a little, and a lot more interesting.

In second grade there were classroom rules hanging from the ceiling. The only one I can remember now seems like it would be a good rule for life. 'Everyone must feel safe.' Safe to be themselves, physically safe, safe to say what they think, just safe. That's the best rule I can think of.

Now I'm in middle school. I guess I've grown up a little, it's all relative anyway, nine years is as long as forty years depending on how long you've lived. I stole that from my dad.

Sometimes I think my dad is the wisest person in the world.

You understand none of this is really true, because what I wrote today is true, but you'll read it by tomorrow, or the next day, and my whole life will be different. Is that how life is, a new draft for every day, a new view for each hour?

When I graduated fifth grade we had a list of questions for our yearbook. One of them was 'What do you want to be when you grow up?' Everyone wrote something like 'doctor' or 'astronaut' or 'Spiderman,' and then you turned the page and there was my five-paragraph manifesto on the million things I wanted to be, from wandering poet to first woman president. That was real cute in fifth grade but when it's ten years later, I'm a junior in college, and I still don't have the conviction to cross 'Spiderman' off my list – well, you can imagine it gets a little nerve-wracking.

My mother used to walk with me to the bottom of the hill to wait for the car pool – I was nervous that I would do it wrong. I remember, or maybe I invent, that occasionally we decided on the way, I wasn't going to school. We stole time that way. She took me to lunch. We went to bookstores in Seattle. She bought me books on love and delinquency, and although she never said it straight out, I'm sure she was hoping I'd become a bank robber. My mother would never admit it, but she wanted me exactly how I turned out – scattered and deviant and too loud.

She changes her clothes.

I'm building the world myself and putting new hats on everybody one by one, before I go out, so wrinkled, I have to grab the great big flaccid flaps of my eyebrows and lift them off my cheekbones in order to see. Before I go out I'm gonna have people in tutus, cops wearing sombreros, stockbrokers with Viking hats, priests with panties on their heads. In the world I'm building, everybody shouts hello to everybody else from their car windows. People have speakers attached to their chests that pour out music so you can tell from a distance what mood they're in, and they won't be too chicken to get naked when the rain comes. And first ladies carry handcuffs and bull whips and presidents wear metal collars. Big metal collars with tight leashes.

She emerges. Barefoot.

Okay. I'm Rachel. Sometimes I wear ripped blue jeans.
Sometimes I wear polyester. Sometimes I take off all my
clothes and swim naked at the beach. I don't believe in fate but
my astrological sign is Aries, the ram, and my sign on the
Chinese zodiac is the sheep, and the name Rachel means sheep
but I've got a fire in my belly. It used to be such a big loud
blazing fire that I couldn't hear anybody else over it. So I talked
a lot and I didn't listen too much. Then I went to middle school
where you gotta be *cool* and you gotta be *strong* and *tough*,
and I tried real hard to be cool. But luckily, luckily I happened
to get a free trip to Russia and I saw another country for the
first time.

In the streets and the alleys it was an obstacle course of garbage
and mud and graffiti. There was coal dust on the snow,
everything was dirty. And they always said to us, 'How do
you like our dirty city?' Oh, but it was so pretty with the little
lights in the windows and the red dusk-light on the buildings.
It was flawed, dirty, broken and gorgeous.

I looked backwards across the Pacific Ocean and from that
distance some things back here in Olympia, Washington, USA
seemed a little weird and disconcerting. But I was awake in
Russia. I was awake for the first time with bug-eyes and a grin.

On the flight home from Anchorage to Seattle everything was
dark. Then the sun began to rise, the water was shining, and
I realized we were flying over Puget Sound. Soon we could see
islands in that water, evergreen trees on those islands.

And I began to sob. I sobbed in all that radiance, in the midst
of the most glorious sunrise I'd ever seen, because it wasn't
enough. It wasn't enough to make me glad to be home.

Maybe it was finally the trees who told me to stay. Or maybe
going to school in my hometown was just the path of least
resistance. Maybe going to Evergreen State College was just
the best way to be different from my Economics-major-high
achiever-khaki-and-high-heels-Yalie-corporate sister and
brother. I don't know why I stayed. But one day I knew I had
to. It was the same day I decided to be an artist and a writer

and I didn't give a shit if I was mediocre and I didn't give a shit if I starved to death and I didn't give a shit if my whole damn high school turned and pointed and laughed in my face.

I was finally awake, forever and ever.

Picking up a print-out.

Yesterday I heard from Chris in Gaza. I am being invited there. I need to go.

I've been organizing in Olympia for a little over a year on anti-war/global justice issues. And it started to feel like this work is missing a connection to the people who are impacted by US foreign policy. I just think we all have the right to be critical of government policies . . . any government policies, particularly policies which we're funding. I feel pretty isolated from the world because of living in Olympia my whole life and my activism at this point has been extremely tied to Olympia. But I've had this underlying need to go to a place and meet people who are on the other end of the tax money that goes to fund the US military. Trying to be local and be respectful of the local is a big part of my ethic, I guess.

What I need to do.

She writes in her notebook.

Send Tuesday's minutes out over the internet.
Write an article for Monday's staff newsletter.
Call Tom again.
Make a list of things hanging over my head.

I am given to making very important lists.

Reading from her notebook.

Five People I Wish I'd Met Who Are Dead:
Salvador Dali
Karl Jung
MLK
JFK
Josephine.

Five People To Hang Out With In Eternity:
Rainer Maria Rilke
Jesus
ee cummings
Gertrude Stein
Zelda Fitzgerald

Six – Charlie Chaplin.

She starts to pack a bag.

I didn't intend to become so deeply involved in activism this year. I'm not sure what compelled me to sign up for the Local Knowledge class – there's such a big degree of community involvement. I'm phobic of community. I'm scared of people, particularly people in the greater Olympia area.

I've been here my whole life. Almost everyone I know and have known in Olympia came from somewhere else.

This is another place where progressive white people escaped a few decades ago – a place where hippie kids come after touring with jam bands.

I don't think my intention was to be of any particular use to the communities we studied. I was looking for curious facts to flesh out an authentic setting. Trivia.

Like – when I worked at Mount Rainier we followed a woman into the woods. She had become part owl. Her job was to entice them out. Our job was to carry the live mice. Somehow, after years of doing spotted owl survey, this woman's larynx changed. She croaked in a language that was articulated somewhere deeper than tonsils. Her tongue must have changed shape. We followed her through the woods on the northwest side of the mountain all day and we saw no owls. And no owls croaked back at her.

I think about how many of us doing any kind of progressive work in this region swim beneath the surface combing for what was here before, and taking inventory of what is now. There's the chance that you will be changed by what you're looking for. Your tongue could change shape like the woman at Rainier.

Studying the history of this area roots me. We've certainly waded in the same water and wandered on the same beaches as very brave people. It makes bravery seem more possible.

We can look at that history and then choose which side we want to be on now, and how willing we are to fight. We are not outside.

Over a thousand people are still, as far as I can tell, being held somewhere in the United States, and it's unclear why. They arrest the 'dirty-bomber,' someone apparently 'in the very early stages' of planning an attack on the US, and this is big news. What does this say about the other thousand people held somewhere? That they weren't in the early stages of planning anything.

Looking for where I fit into all this forced me out into the community.

You come to take for granted where you belong in a town. If you have an overactive fantasy life you just start making things up. You can remember just enough unrelated pieces of trivia to hold up coffee-table conversation and never have to think about anything disturbing or demanding of action.

I'm still pretty shell-shocked by this semester. I spoke to a room of about forty international students. I've helped in the planning of two conferences, facilitated meetings, danced down the street with forty people from the ages of seven to seventy, dressed as doves. I spent a lot of time with the homeless group. I went with them to the city council. I went to the community conversation. I slept out overnight on Mayday.

Who is this person? How did I get here?

I will not leave the house if it's to turn in my own work or complete some other act of self-preservation. I will never leave my bed.

The salmon talked me into a lifestyle change. There's a hole, a pipe, in the bulkhead at the East Bay Marina. Every year salmon swim into that hole, trying to get back home. Salmon have to make it all the way up Plum Street in that hole. That hole is Moxlie Creek.

Once you know that there are salmon down there it's hard to forget. You imagine their moony eyes while you walk home from the bar in your slutty boots. It's hard to be extraordinarily vacuous when you always have the salmon in the back of your mind: in that pipe down there – on their way to daylight at Watershed Park. Salmon are the history that isn't trivia. They are what was here before.

I look at this place now and I just want to do right by it. The salmon beneath downtown and the creeks and the inlets and the people who were here first and my elementary school teachers and my mom.

Leaving a phone message.

Hey Mom, could you e-mail to me with anyone you know who it would be good to contact if I get in trouble – though I'm not planning on it – friends or family who would call their Congress people, etc. – also, friends who might be interested in getting info or at least knowing that I'm going?

I'm going to give *The Olympian* your number. Please think about your language when you talk to them. I think it was smart that you're wary of using the word 'terrorism', and if you talk about the cycle of violence, or 'an eye for an eye', you could be perpetuating the idea that the Israeli-Palestinian conflict is a balanced conflict, instead of a largely unarmed people against the fourth most powerful military in the world. These are the kind of things it's important to think about before talking to reporters.

I'll call you tonight.

We have a very involved mother . . . overly involved sometimes. This means we have to claw our way toward autonomy – kick and scream and yell to get some space to grow in. It also means we let her take care of things we are capable of doing ourselves.

I think of my mom as being extremely moralistic. Not in a bad way. Just there were things that none of us did. Lying, teasing, taking things, just being rude to people. Sometimes she wondered if we would be healthier, better children if she had taken us to church. This may have been a scare tactic of hers.

I know a woman who's pregnant and she's decided not to assign a gender to her baby until it chooses its own. I think that's a little nuts. Anyway, I think maybe my mom had a similar attitude toward my spirituality. She was determined I would define it for myself.

I could write a history of my family according to discoveries I've made over the years in cupboards and drawers. Unfinished baby books. Duplicate containers of oregano from houses I lived in and moved out of, taking the seasoning with me. Placemats that defeated cranberry juice and oyster stew and candle wax.

I am heartbroken when I search in my mother's drawers. I am heartbroken by the way she arranges jewelery. I know she returns her earrings to their little boxes when she finishes with them. I am heartbroken at the thought of her, standing in her big bra and her pantyhose stretched over her underwear, dabbing on lipstick, moving pink powder across the bones of her cheeks, rubbing it into her pores until it hangs on. My mother ages and puts on make-up – slides bracelets across her wrists – where the skin is loose.

Sometimes my mother is up there, bobbing in the sky like Macy's Parade balloons. Sometimes my mother is so big she looms over everything.

Finding a photograph of Cindy, her mother.

I know I scare you, Mom.

I'm sorry I scare you. But I want to write and I want to see. And what would I write about if I only stayed within the doll's house, the flower-world I grew up in?

You gave me a potential.

I love you but I'm growing out of what you gave me. I'm saving it inside me and growing outwards. Let me fight my monsters. You made me. You made me.

Packing photograph of Cindy.

Mom, why doesn't Dad ever write to me? Has he gotten himself addicted to cocaine while he's away and forgotten about his family? He never wrote back to me and gave me fatherly advice about how to get a job . . . or told me how he almost got swept into the ocean looking for whelks. If this continues I'm going to have to start dating 40-year-old men to make up for my underdeveloped animus.

Actually, Dad, that was just a little joke, but I think it is important that I fill you in on some sketchy things that have been going on up here. Don't tell Mom who tipped you off, but the mailman's been coming by a lot more than usual, and staying for a real long time, and wearing really racy high-cut mailman shorts. And Mom's been dressing real trampy. I just thought you should know.

RACHEL *as Craig, her father.*

'You're just like your mother. Making fun of people with disabilities. You criticize me for not writing when I can hardly see the computer, let alone the type on its screen. Now that I have reading glasses, my wife says they make my eyes look too big. Yet I understand your criticism. I should have written you, sighted or not, it's no excuse. Never mind that all I get is the hand-me-downs. The cast-off e-mails written to your mother that she may choose to share with her husband. Or not. But I don't complain. It's a father's life: work all day so that others may enjoy. I give it freely. Never a word from me!'

RACHEL *to Craig.*

You never get your own personal e-mails because if I so much as give you a 'heads up' in one of my e-mails to Mom, I have to prepare myself for the mockery and neo-liberal jabs at my progressive education that are always the thanks I get. Down, oppressor man!

To the audience.

Incidentally, at this point, the neo-liberal jabs are pretty close to the mark. At one lecture, our guest speaker was, I think, a physicist. But his side occupation is dream-work. 'Hi, my name is Dr Jenson, I'm a Harvard grad with a PhD in Political Economy, but on the side I analyze the paintings of my pet donkey, Aphrodite.'

I like my class. The reading is very interesting. The schedule is completely indecipherable. And the teachers wrap themselves in paper, sing in German, and yell insults at us to help us get a grasp on Dadaism.

To Craig.

It's a good thing that you, Chris and Sarah all appear to have stable salaries, because I am steadfastly pursuing a track that guarantees I'll never get paid more than three Triscuits and some spinach.

RACHEL *packs Craig's photograph.*

Packing away bed, books, etc.

What I have –
a house cat.
small hands, crooked toes, knees, elbows
thighs, a throat and a belly.
dirt under my nails.
six lost journals underneath seats
in trains across the country
a Buick. questionable.
eight black ballpoint pens
sharp teeth
beady eyes
and hope.

What I want –
a garden with pumpkins
and bare earth to turn over and
turn over
hardwood floors for sock ballets
air and raspberries
sometimes in the morning
danger and stolen kisses
from a sneaky mystery lover man.

Picking up a photograph of Colin.

I have exactly as much of Colin's memory as I need. The sun
was shining, Colin read political economy in the green chair.
I danced around to Magnetic Fields and mowed the lawn.

We walked to school together in the morning, and finally it
rained. Colin wanted me to walk faster. Colin always wanted to
walk faster, and I wanted to trudge and identify ferns.

I woke up early one day with errands to run and decided I would bump into Colin and his new hoochie-ass girlfriend. I shaved my armpits. I danced around in front of the mirror in the tight shirt I got in the little boy's section of the Salvation Army. I smeared on ChapStick.

'Fun life,' I say, 'Fun life.' I imagine I live in a Mountain Dew commercial. I am always on the beach with a bevy of sinewed friends and we're always dancing.

I meander through downtown. They are here somewhere, most likely in a shadow, ensnared together. They'll drop the spoons in their strawberry milkshake when I slide past. Free as a bird. Fun life. Toucan Sam.

They are not at the coffee shop. They are not in the grocery store, on the bridge, at the magazine stand. I drive to the school, embarrassed at myself. Of course he emerges from the library. Minus hoochie-ass girlfriend. I shove my hips out in the sun and make six-guns. He makes six-guns back at me. This town ain't big enough for the two of us.

'Hey-hey.'

'Hey-hey.'

'What are you doing here?'

'Reading up on some young anarchists.'

He pronounces his words like rubber bands stretched and snapping. I perform a dance beneath the conversation, like I have to pee.

Fun life. Fun life. Fun life.

'How are you?'

He's uncomfortable. I grin, sunshine on the apples of my cheeks.

'Well. I'm well. Meeting some people.'

I'm always on the beach with a bevy of sinewed friends.

'How are you?'

'Good. Gotta job scrubbing toilets.'

'Nice!'

'My friend from North Carolina went home.'

'You had a friend here from North Carolina?'

'You know – Leslie.'

Sunshine on the apples of my cheeks, sticky in my eyelashes and I'm on the beach and I'm always dancing.

'Shit, Colin! What happened? But things were going so well!'

He shook his head. Laughed at me.

It is easy to make the journey. You will know when the time comes. You will fall in love with someone who is perpetually leaving you. Someone who beats you at Scrabble and talks with big words and tells all stories as if they are blues songs. You will memorize the features of someone whose eyes are perpetually bored and whose lips are perpetually amused.

Eventually, I convinced Colin to quit drowning out my life. The topography of his life consisted of emergency adrenaline shots, jail, sometimes near-death experiences. The topography of my life consisted of making up names for the neighborhood cats, on some days a small new poem, the gossip among my friends. His life was skyscrapers. My life took place on a much smaller scale. That is done now. We are proportionate.

Putting on her shoes and socks.

On Wednesday I walked into the forest. Down the path to the little wooden bridge over the creek. And I stood on the bridge and looked at a log that lay across the little stream. Someone had taken rocks from the stream and lined them up like little multicolored frogs across the log.

I took off my boots and my socks and set them down on the edge of the bridge. Then I jumped onto the bank and climbed onto that log and walked across it, barefoot, nimbly, so that only one of the rocks fell into the water. I squatted in the pebbles and fished interesting rocks out of the stream for myself. I cleaned them and held them and put them in my pocket. Then I stood like Huck Finn with my jeans rolled up, with my back to the bridge and my two empty little brown boots. I sang to the forest. I hummed. I made up waltzes. I belted out Russian drinking songs. Opened my mouth wide and sang.

She sings.

Leaving Olympia.

We are all born and someday we'll all die. Most likely to some degree alone.

What if our aloneness isn't a tragedy? What if our aloneness is what allows us to speak the truth without being afraid? What if our aloneness is what allows us to adventure – to experience the world as a dynamic presence – as a changeable, interactive thing?

If I lived in Bosnia or Rwanda or who knows where else, needless death wouldn't be a distant symbol to me, it wouldn't be a metaphor, it would be a reality.

And I have no right to this metaphor. But I use it to console myself. To give a fraction of meaning to something enormous and needless.

This realization. This realization that I will live my life in this world where I have privileges.

I can't cool boiling waters in Russia. I can't be Picasso. I can't be Jesus. I can't save the planet single-handedly.

I can wash dishes.

Arriving in Jerusalem.

January 25th, 2003.

Very little problem at the airport. My tight jeans and cropped bunny-hair sweater seem to have made all the difference – and of course the use of my Israeli friend's address. The only question was, 'Where did you meet her?' The woman behind the glass appeared not to notice my shaking hands. I took a shared taxi into Jerusalem and noticed that the Holy Land is full of rocks and it seems like driving, you could fall off these hills. Just before we leave the airport I read, in the *Let's Go Israel* book, that more Israelis have been killed in car accidents than in all of Israel's wars combined.

Writing in notebook.

Things to do:
Buy phone card
Buy phone
E-mail Michael
Call Joe & Gili
Change money
Call Mom with cell number.

My introduction to curfew was gentle: a rush outside in the midst of our training to buy lunch before the shops closed in Beit Sahour. There was music – singing in Arabic – pouring into the street from somewhere. By the time the whole group of us had shawarma and falafel, the noise had become the bleat of military jeep horns, the squeal of a car and a voice shouting through a bullhorn – border police or IDF, I don't remember which. As the training went on, there was noise and flashing lights outside – but it wasn't real for me somehow because I was inside this building with these people. Everyone extending theories into the air.

The scariest thing for non-Jewish Americans in talking about Palestinian self-determination is the fear of being or sounding anti-Semitic. The people of Israel are suffering and Jewish people have a long history of oppression. We still have some responsibility for that, but I think it's important to draw a firm distinction between the policies of Israel as a state, and Jewish people. That's kind of a no-brainer, but there is very strong pressure to conflate the two. I try to ask myself, whose interest does it serve to identify Israeli policy with all Jewish people?

Anyway, this kind of stuff I just think about all the time and my ideas evolve. I'm really new to talking about Israel-Palestine, so I don't always know the political implications of my words.

Reading from her notebook.

Notes from Training:
When Talking – no hearsay. Call hospitals and official sources. Use quotes. Don't appear to judge rightness or wrongness. Non-Violence – Don't touch those we're confronting. Don't run. Carry nothing that could be used as a weapon. No self-initiating actions.

January 26th.

Travel from Beit Sahour to Jerusalem.

January 27th.

An attack in Gaza the night before last killed fourteen and injured around thirty.

The West Bank and Gaza are under extremely strict curfew until after the election tomorrow. You are not allowed to leave your house at all. Not for food. Nothing. I am still in Jerusalem aiming to get to Rafah to join the other internationals trying to prevent the demolition of civilian homes.

I am relatively sheltered here. Walking around with Palestinians I wait while they are stopped to show ID. Blue stars of David are spray-painted on doors in the Arab section of the old city. I have never seen that symbol used in quite that way. I am used to seeing the *cross* used in a colonialist way. I know this is something I can't really understand, right now. The reality of curfew, of the checkpoints. I'm sort of embarrassed about how long it takes me to realize in my gut that people live like this . . .

Reading from her notebook.

At 10pm, I travel to Rafah. Jehan met the cab. Soldiers at bus stations. Bombed market in Gaza City. Children grab my ass, throw garbage at my head, scream, 'What's your name?'

Writing in her notebook.

Sleep in tent. Gunshot through tent. Start smoking.

January 31st.

Today I decided to follow Joe's lead and write in every spare
crack of time in every day. I always regret the blank space in
my journal from Russia. Here it is different. I am older and the
world does not revolve around me. We are in Jehan's brother's
apartment in Khan Younis.

The neighborhoods that have asked us for some form of
presence are Yibna, Tel El Sultan, Hi Salam, Brazil, Block J,
Zorob, and Block O.

There is some visible class difference between this building in
Khan Younis and, say, Brazil or Block J. There are toys for the
children. A table. But this apartment – with blank walls and
birds weaving in and out of the windows – would be
symptomatic of nearly crushing poverty in the United States.

There is greenery here. Some trees and grassy places – maybe
it is shielded a little by Rafah which is razed and bullet-riddled
and bare. Jehan's uncle came to sit with us. He told us that
there was a peaceful time in the late '70s and early '80s. 'We
build their buildings. We work in the factory.' He says it is the
leaders that make war.

Writing in her journal.

Today. Visits to –
Gaza, re: Nursing
UN
Children's Parliament
Women's group.

We need to make:
One beautiful banner in Arabic and English.

February 1st.

After we'd helped the water people do more repairs we had gone to look for banner fabric. Jehan found Will and me waiting to pay the man for 30 meters of white cotton. She told us someone had been killed at the Rafah/Egypt border. We met up at the apartment and rode in a strangely Californian SUV past the cemetery to the Palestinian side of the border. A swarm of people waited there. We were given a stretcher and ushered into an office. People talked for a while and then we went out – each of us with a handle.

We started into the field: five internationals plus Jehan. Jenny spoke over the bullhorn saying, 'Do not shoot. We are unarmed civilians,' naming the countries we came from and letting the IDF know our intention to retrieve this man's body.

The first response from the IDF was shouting, 'Go back.' Then they shot about 20 meters in front of us.

As we continued to walk in the direction of the body – the shots shifted – hitting the ground two to four meters in front of us. We also heard two high-pitched, whistling shots above our heads. We stopped and Jenny requested to talk to the commanding officer.

A white truck with a blue light rolled up and the person in the truck spoke over the loudspeaker. Told us to leave. Stated, 'You'll get the body later.'

The white truck cruised away.

Then a tank and a bulldozer emerged from the IDF side of the checkpoint and proceeded toward the olive grove. They began moving dirt between us and the olive grove. Smoke blew.

They created a mound of dirt and shot repeatedly into it.

This is my very poor drawing of the dead body we just carried. He had a big white hand poised in the air off the stretcher as if doing the crawl or throwing a baseball.

Had a dream about falling, falling to my death off of something dusty and smooth and crumbling like the cliffs in Utah, but I kept holding on, and when each new foothold or handle of rock broke, I reached out as I fell and grabbed a new one. I didn't have time to think about anything – just react as if I was playing an adrenaline-filled video game. And I heard, 'I can't die, I can't die,' again and again in my head. Seems somehow positive compared to the dreams I used to have of tumbling, thinking, 'This is it, I'm going to die.'

Reading from her notebook.

February 4th.

In Dr Samir's garden.

Fig tree with small buds. Dill, lettuce, garlic.
White plastic chairs, deflated soccer ball, blanket drying on
a line.
Patchy lawn, long shadows.
Two bulldozers, tanks.

I went to the kitchen and stayed two hours. The tank stayed
too, so no work, no school.

A soldier came with a sledgehammer.
The tank started firing – the family were watching *Tom &
Jerry* in the kitchen.
I played with the children to distract them.

Dr Samir says, 'Before intifada – no tanks, no bulldozers, no
gunshots, no noise.
After intifada, daily. Gunshots daily.
I have no gun in my house, nothing.
30 years collecting money for house.
We also afraid no other place to go, three hours they can
destroy house.
I look at my garden. I ask myself, "This year will you eat from
these trees like other years?" – I trust in my god – so no
problem.'

February 6th.

I rode on the bulldozer as it repaired the road throughout the day. Jenny and Will held a banner and spoke through the megaphone for us. A tank stayed present throughout the action. And at some point a jeep arrived. This frightened me because I know at least one person was shot by soldiers in a green jeep.

Some youths – maybe three – came out toward the banner, and then soldiers got out of the jeep and shot toward the internationals. Jehan found bits of shrapnel later in her shoes.

Rafah
Ghost homes
Glow-in-the-dark stars in teenagers' bedrooms
Tumbling of concrete
Constant anonymous night-vision telescope.

February 7th.

I have been in Palestine for two weeks and one hour now, and I still have very few words to describe what I see. I don't know if many of the children here have ever existed without tank-shell holes in their walls. I think even the smallest of these children understand that life is not like this everywhere. They love to get me to practise my limited Arabic. Today I tried to learn to say, 'Bush is a tool', but I don't think it translated quite right. But anyway, there are eight-year-olds here more aware of the workings of the global power structure than I was just a few years ago – at least regarding Israel.

Nothing could have prepared me for the reality of the situation here. You just can't imagine it unless you see it. And even then your experience is not at all the reality: what with the difficulties the Israeli army would face if they shot an unarmed US citizen, the fact that I have money to buy water when the army destroys wells, and of course, the fact that I have the option of leaving. I am allowed to see the ocean.

If I feel outrage at entering briefly into the world in which these children exist, I wonder how it would be for them to arrive in my world. Once you have seen the ocean and lived in a silent place where water is taken for granted and not stolen in the night by bulldozers, spent an evening when you didn't wonder if the walls of your home might suddenly fall inward, aren't surrounded by towers, tanks, and now a giant metal wall, I wonder if you can forgive the world for all the years spent existing – just existing – in resistance to the constant attempt to erase you from your home. That is something I wonder about these children. I wonder what would happen if they really knew.

I am in Rafah. A city of 140,000 people, 60% of whom are refugees – many twice or three times over. Currently, the Israeli army is building a twelve-meter-high wall between Rafah and the border. 602 homes have been completely bulldozed and the number partially destroyed is greater.

Today, as I walked on top of the rubble, Egyptian soldiers called to me from the other side of the border: 'Go! Go!' because a tank was coming. And then waving and 'What's your name?' Something disturbing about this friendly curiosity. To some degree, we are all kids curious about other kids. Egyptian kids shouting at strange women wandering into the path of tanks. Palestinian kids shot from the tanks when they peek out from behind walls to see what's going on. International kids standing in front of tanks with banners. Israeli kids in the tanks – occasionally shouting, occasionally waving – many forced to be here, many just aggressive, anonymously shooting into the houses as we wander away.

In addition to tanks, there are more IDF towers than I can count. Some just army-green metal, others these strange spiral staircases draped in some kind of netting. A new one went up the other day in the time it took us to do laundry and cross town twice to hang banners. And nowhere invulnerable to Apache helicopters or the cameras of invisible drones we hear buzzing over the city for hours at a time.

We've been wavering between five and six of us internationals. There are requests for constant nighttime presence at a well on the outskirts of Rafah since the two largest wells were destroyed last week, but after about 10pm it is very difficult to move because the Israeli army treats anyone in the streets as resistance and shoots at them. So clearly we are too few.

I went to a rally a few days ago in Khan Younis in solidarity with the people of Iraq. Many analogies were made about the continuing suffering of the Palestinian people and the upcoming occupation of Iraq by the United States – not the war itself, but the certain aftermath of the war.

People here watch the media, and they told me again today that there have been large protests in the United States and 'problems for the government' in the UK. So now I don't feel like a complete Pollyanna when I tell people that not everyone in the United States supports the policies of our government.

I'm just beginning to learn from what I expect to be a very intense tutelage in the ability of people to organize against all odds, and to resist against all odds.

I knew a few years ago what the unbearable lightness was, before I read the book. The lightness – between life and death, there are no dimensions at all. There are no rulers or mile-markers. It's just a shrug – the difference between Hitler and my mother, the difference between Whitney Houston and a Russian mother watching her son fall through the sidewalk and boil to death. There are no rules. There is no fairness. There are no guarantees. No warranties on anything. It's all just a shrug, the difference between ecstasy and misery is just a shrug. And with that enormous shrug there, the shrug between being and not being – how could I be a poet? How could I believe in a truth?

And I knew, back then, that the shrug would happen at the end of my life – I knew. And I thought, so who cares? If my whole life is going to amount to one shrug and a shake of the head, who cares if it comes in eighty years or at 8pm? Who cares?

Now, I know who cares. I know if I die at 11.15pm or at 97 years – I know. And I know it's me. That's my job.

Reading from her notebook.

February 11th.

Tufah Checkpoint.
Women and kids on right, men on left, ID passes in their hands.
The women with babies and buckets – all middle-aged.

At 2pm they said the checkpoint would open.
2.40pm – it opens.

Six old men proceed, then the IDF announces only five at a time.
Then came five women with four children and a baby in arms.

A soldier runs forward, yelling.
The women kneel, stand up again, and return.

3pm – five or six men go through.
3.04pm – five more.

3.10pm – the group of women and children proceed again.
3.25pm – five men waiting.

February 20th.

Both of the major checkpoints are closed. This means that
Palestinians who want to go and register for their next quarter
at university can't. People can't get to their jobs; those who are
trapped on the other side can't get home; and internationals,
who have a meeting tomorrow in the West Bank, won't make
it. We could if we made serious use of our international white-
person privilege, but that would also mean some risk of arrest
and deportation, even though none of us have done anything
illegal.

I am staying put in Rafah for now, no plans to head north.
A lot of very nice Palestinians are looking after me. I have
a small flu bug and got some lemony drinks to cure me. Also,
the woman who keeps the key for the well where we still sleep
keeps asking about my mom – wants to make sure I'm calling
you.

She goes to the computer.

Checking e-mails.

Rachel,

I am very concerned for you. But I know most of this is not about you, but about the people, the families you are building solidarity with. I have worried a little, because it seems to me that it could be easy to be manipulated by one faction or another. For myself, I feel like I'm fighting a lifetime of indoctrination. Palestinians have really been invisible to me, but you are changing that.

In regards to Palestinian violence, I just abhor any violence. I understand that most are just trying feebly to defend themselves, but here, just the mention of suicide bombing puts up a wall.

There is a lot in my heart but I am having trouble with the words. Be safe, be well. Do you think about coming home? Because of war and all? I know probably not, but I hope you feel it would be okay if you did.

Mama.

She replies.

February 28th.

Mom,

I spent the evening and this morning with a family on the front line in Hi Salam – who fixed me dinner – and have cable TV. The two front rooms of their house are unusable because gunshots have been fired through the walls, so the whole family sleep in the parents' bedroom. I sleep on the floor next to the youngest daughter and we all share blankets. I helped the son with his English homework a little, and we all watched *Pet Sematary*, which is a horrifying movie. They all thought it was pretty funny how much trouble I had watching it. Friday is the holiday, and when I woke up they were watching *Gummi Bears* dubbed into Arabic. So I ate breakfast with them and sat there for a while and just enjoyed being in this big puddle of blankets with this family watching what for me seemed like Saturday morning cartoons.

Then I walked some way to Brazil Block, which is where the big family live, the one that has wholeheartedly adopted me. The other day, the grandmother gave me a lecture that involved a lot of blowing and pointing to her black shawl. I got Nidal to tell her that my mother would appreciate knowing that someone here was giving me a hard time about smoking turning my lungs black.

I am amazed at their strength in defending such a large degree of their humanity against the incredible horror occurring in their lives and against the constant presence of death. I think the word is dignity.

Of course, we burn out. Of course, it is overwhelming. Whenever I organize or participate in public protest I get really worried that it will just suck, be really small, embarrassing, and the media will laugh at us. Oftentimes it is really small and most of the time the media does laugh at us and of course it doesn't get coverage all over the world, but in some places the word 'Rafah' is mentioned outside of the Arab press. If the international media and our government are not going to tell us that we are effective, valuable, we have to do that for each other, and one way we can do that is by continuing our work, visibly.

I look forward to seeing more and more people willing to resist the direction the world is moving in: a direction where our personal experiences are irrelevant, that we are defective, that our communities are not important, that we are powerless, that the future is determined, and that the highest level of humanity is expressed through what we choose to buy at the mall.

Maybe you should try to get Dad to quit his neo-liberal job and become a Math teacher. Maybe you should try to get him to sabotage his neo-liberal job. Do you think he could accidentally dump a lot of dollars very cheaply into international markets? Okay. Sorry. I love you guys. Take care of yourselves.

Writing in notebook.

Set up system for media work
Prepare paragraph for rally
Go to Block J and investigate home
Stay and work tonight
Call Dr Samir.

Checking e-mail.

Todd!

Reading e-mail.

Hey you!

Keep up the strength. It is much needed in this world. You really make me want to go there.

She replies.

Holy shit, Todd – come here! The work we do needs people who know how to support this community, not just start our own separate 'international solidarity show'. The people here are incredible.

Come here come here come here come here come here come here come here come here come here come here.

Writing in her notebook.

Call Gili for talk with Alice
Plan for Women's Day
Saturday am – choose new house.

At the computer.

March 1st.

10.30am – three internationals joined four men at the El Iskan water well. It provides 25% of Rafah's water supply.

Workers at the well reported being fired upon on Thursday.

Despite guarantees of safety and presence of banners and megaphones, activists and workers were fired on several times over a period of one hour, close enough to spray debris in their faces.

For information about the report and other issues related to the destruction of civilian water supplies in Rafah, please contact Rachel.

Writing in her notebook.

We need:
Battery-charged striplights
Megaphone
Lamps
Fabric
Envelopes.

Checking e-mail.

Dad . . .

She reads.

Rachel,

I find writing to you hard, but not thinking about you impossible. So I don't write, but I do bore my friends at lunch, giving vent to my fear. I am afraid for you, and I think I have reason to be. But I'm also proud of you – very proud. But as Don Remfert says: I'd just as soon be proud of somebody else's daughter. That's how fathers are: we're hard-wired not to want our children, no matter how old they are, no matter how brave they are, and no matter how much good they are doing, to be subject to so much threat or even to witness so much suffering. You may say (have said) that it is wrong for me to stick my head in the sand; but I say I am only trying to (or just wishing

I could) stick your head in the sand – and that's different. Hard-wired. Can't be changed on that aspect of the issue.

She replies.

Hi Papa,

I feel like sometimes I spend all my time propagandizing Mom, and assuming that she'll pass stuff on to you, so you get neglected. Don't worry about me too much, right now I am most concerned that we are not being effective. I still don't feel particularly at risk.

I am trying to figure out what I'm going to do when I leave here.

One of the core members of our group has to leave tomorrow, and watching her say goodbye is making me realize how difficult it will be. People here can't leave, so that complicates things. They are also pretty matter-of-fact about whether or not they will be alive when we come back here. I really don't want to live with a lot of guilt about this place – being able to come and go so easily. I know I should try and link up with the family in France, but I think that I'm not going to do that. I would just be angry, and not much fun to be around. It seems like a transition into too much opulence right now – I would feel a lot of class guilt the whole time.

Let me know if you have any ideas about what I should do with the rest of my life. If you want, you can write to me as if I was on vacation at a camp on Hawaii learning to weave. One thing I do to make things easier here is to utterly retreat into fantasies that I am in a Hollywood movie, or a sitcom starring Michael J. Fox. So feel free to make something up and I'll be happy to play along.

I remember the morning I walked with Colin to Puget Pantry
to get cigarettes and a few last-minute prizes for a bingo game
at work. It was my last day as 'drop-ins coordinator' at
Behavioral Health Resources – a community service for
mental-health clients. We met once a week to develop social
skills.

I convinced Colin to walk with me because Puget Pantry had
'The Who's Tommy Pinball'.

On the radio the announcers were talking about giving blood.

I asked the man behind the counter what happened.

'Two towers. Someone bomb.'

'Someone bombed the World Trade Center?'

'Airplanes.'

Colin and I sat on the sidewalk beneath the payphone. We
thought it might be World War III. I called my dad.

I figured if it was World War III, being 'drop-ins coordinator'
was a damn fine situation to go out in.

I look at things the wrong way. I know I do. I know how it
feels not to be normal, though. I don't know how it feels to
have voices or to sleep in those beds with the white knitted
blankets. But yeah, those times when you just know the whole
world is out there, patting their stomachs and saying, 'God
bless us, every one.' And you're inside with the box of blue
plastic gloves for cooking and the no-self-harm contracts and
the antibacterial hand-cleanser.

How you survive in a nonexistent place.

Make a list:
God
breakfast cereal
the prophet Mohammed
play bus
weapons of mass destruction
corner grocery
tawdry affair
Mel Gibson
sandstorm
venereal disease
malnutrition
proxy government
water contamination

Choices:
1. Go back to Olympia.
Finish school. Talk or presentations about Gaza. Clean out my stuff from Sarah's garage.

2. Go to Egypt or Dubai for a year.
Earn money, learn Arabic. Come back to Palestine.

3. Go to Sweden for one month.
Potentially horrible. Go broke.

4. Try to stay in Rafah.
Money? Productivity?

5. Travel elsewhere.

I think my soul is nomadic. I've always turned my head a little to listen out of one ear to the people speaking in Spanish behind me on the bus. I've always stared upward at airplanes cutting white paths through the sky and wondered where they're going. I've always been jealous of migratory birds.

In a year or two, or maybe next winter, I'll go to South America.

I will smile across the water at the Olympics. When I leave, I'll ride up over the rises and dips of that road that I've been riding over all my life, through the cedars and past the barn. I'll lean out the window when I pass my old high school and scream, 'Ha Ha Ha! Fuck You! Fuck You!' just for old times' sake. I'll get on Highway 101 and when it reaches I-5, I'll either go north towards the airport or south towards Mexico.

When I leave, I'll leave laughing. I'll come back to see my mother and my college friends and to swim naked in Puget Sound at night. And I won't be afraid to come back, like I've always been afraid before. I'll cry, but I'll be smiling, and I'll hug my mom.

She goes to the computer.

March 9th.

Today's Demo.
At least ten greenhouses destroyed. Cucumbers, peas, olives, tomatoes.
Quiet area. 300 people dependent on farms to live.
150-200 men arrested.
Shot around them. Beat them. Six people in hospital.

They don't understand what has happened.

March 13th, 9pm.

Intensive care unit – 12-year-old girl shot from tower in school near Nasser hospital.

11pm – shooting behind West Camp.
Came from settlement into main market – two or three Apaches.

Evacuated apartment building – eight families.

Shot inside hospital – three injured – nurses.

6am – houses demolished.

41 injured.

Mom.

I have bad nightmares about tanks and bulldozers outside our house, and you and me inside. Sometimes the adrenaline acts as an anesthetic for weeks – and then at night it just hits me again a little bit of the reality of the situation. I am really scared for the people here. Yesterday I watched a father lead his two tiny children holding his hand out into the sight of tanks and a sniper tower and bulldozers because he thought his house was going to be exploded.

It was our mistake in translation that made him think this, although I'm sure it is only a matter of time. In fact, the Israeli army was in the process of detonating an explosive in the ground nearby. This is in the area where Sunday about 150 men were rounded up outside the settlement with gunfire over their heads, while tanks and bulldozers destroyed twenty-five greenhouses – the livelihoods of three hundred people. To think that this man felt it was less of a risk to walk out in view of the tanks with his kids than to stay in his house. I was really scared that they were all going to be shot, and I tried to stand between them and the tank. This happens every day, but this father walking out with his two little kids just looking very sad, happened to get my attention more at this particular moment, probably because I felt like it was our translation problems that made him leave.

I thought a lot about what you said about Palestinian violence not helping the situation. 60,000 people from Rafah worked in Israel two years ago. Now only 600 can go there for jobs. Of these 600, many have moved, because the three checkpoints make a 40-minute drive into a 12-hour or impassable journey.

Sources of economic growth are all completely destroyed – the airport (runways demolished, totally closed); the border for trade with Egypt (now with a sniper tower in the middle of the crossing); access to the ocean (completely cut off in the last two years).

There used to be a middle class here – recently. We get reports that in the past, Gazan flower shipments to Europe were delayed for two weeks for security inspections. You can imagine the value of two-week-old cut flowers, so that market dried up. And then the bulldozers come and take out vegetable farms and gardens. What is left for people? Tell me if you can think of anything. I can't.

So when someone says that any act of Palestinian violence justifies Israel's actions not only do I question that logic in light of international law and the right of people to legitimate armed struggle in defence of their land and their families; not only do I question that logic in light of the fourth Geneva Convention which prohibits collective punishment, prohibits the transfer of an occupying country's population into an occupied area, prohibits the expropriation of water resources and the destruction of civilian infrastructure such as farms; not only do I question that logic in light of the notion that fifty-year-old Russian guns and homemade explosives can have any impact on the activities of one of the world's largest militaries, backed by the world's only superpower, I also question that logic on the basis of common sense.

If any of us had our lives and welfare completely strangled and lived with children in a shrinking place where we knew that soldiers and tanks and bulldozers could come for us at any moment, with no means of economic survival and our houses demolished; if they came and destroyed all the greenhouses that we'd been cultivating for the last however long do you not think, in a similar situation, most people would defend themselves as best they could?

You asked me about non-violent resistance, and I mentioned the first intifada. The vast majority of Palestinians right now, as far as I can tell, are engaging in Gandhian non-violent resistance. Who do you think I'm staying with, in houses that are going to be demolished amid gunfire? Who do you think are staffing the human-rights centers? What do you think this Palestinian-led movement is that I joined that engages in non-violent direct action? Who do you think these families are that I tell you about, who won't take any money from us even though they are very, very poor, and who say to us: 'We are not a hotel. We help you because we think maybe you will go and tell people in your country that you lived with Muslims. We think they will know that we are good people. We are quiet people. We just want peace'? Do you think I'm hanging out with Hamas fighters? These people are being shot at every day and they continue to go about their business as best they can in the sights of machine guns and rocket launchers. Isn't that basically the epitome of non-violent resistance?

When that explosive detonated yesterday it broke all the windows in the family's house. I was in the process of being served tea and playing with the two small babies.

I'm having a hard time right now. Just feel sick to my stomach from being doted on very sweetly, by people who are facing doom. I know that from the United States it all sounds like hyperbole. A lot of the time the kindness of the people here, coupled with the willful destruction of their lives, makes it seem unreal to me. I can't believe that something like this can happen in the world without a bigger outcry. It hurts me, again, like it has hurt me in the past, to witness how awful we can allow the world to be.

For a long time I've been operating from a certain core assumption that we are all essentially the same inside, and that our differences are by and large situational. That goes for everybody – Bush, Bin Laden, Tony Blair, me, you, Sarah, Chris, Dad, Gram, Palestinians, everybody of any particular religion. I know there is a good chance that this assumption actually is false. But it's convenient, because it always leads to questions about the way privilege shelters people from the consequences of their actions. It's also convenient because it leads to some level of forgiveness, whether justified or not.

It is my own selfishness and will to optimism that wants to believe that even people with a great deal of privilege don't just idly sit by and watch. What we are paying for here is truly evil. Maybe the general growing class imbalance in the world and consequent devastation of working people's lives is a bigger evil. Being here should make me more aware of what it means to be a farmer in Colombia, for example. Anyway, I'm rambling. Just want to tell my mom that I'm really scared, and questioning my fundamental belief in the goodness of human nature. This has to stop. I think it is a good idea for us all to drop everything and devote our lives to making this stop. I don't think it's an extremist thing to do any more. I still really want to dance around to Pat Benatar and have boyfriends and make comics for my co-workers. But I also want this to stop. Disbelief and horror is what I feel. Disappointment. I am disappointed that this is the base reality of our world and that we, in fact, participate in it. This is not at all what I asked for when I came into this world. This is not at all what the people here asked for when they came into this world. This is not what they are asking for now. This is not the world you and Dad wanted me to come into when you decided to have me. This is not what I meant when I was two and looked at Capitol Lake and said, 'This is the wide world and I'm coming to it.'

When I come back from Palestine I probably will have nightmares and constantly feel guilty for not being here, but I can channel that into more work. Coming here is one of the better things I've ever done.

I love you and Dad. Sorry for the diatribe.

A door opens.

Okay, some strange men are offering me some peas, so I need to eat and thank them.

She leaves.

Rachel Corrie

was killed in Gaza by an Israeli bulldozer on March 16th, 2003.

Epilogue

Rachel Corrie (aged ten).
Remarks from Fifth Grade Press Conference on World Hunger.

'I'm here for other children.
I'm here because I care.
I'm here because children everywhere are suffering and
because forty thousand people die each day from hunger.
I'm here because those people are mostly children.
We have got to understand that the poor are all around us and
we are ignoring them.
We have got to understand that these deaths are preventable.
We have got to understand that people in Third World
countries think and care and smile and cry just like us.
We have got to understand that they dream our dreams and we
dream theirs.
We have got to understand that they are us. We are them.
My dream is to stop hunger by the year 2000.
My dream is to give the poor a chance.
My dream is to save the forty thousand people who die each day.
My dream can and will come true if we all look into the future
and see the light that shines there.
If we ignore hunger, that light will go out.
If we all help and work together, it will grow and burn free
with the potential of tomorrow.'

A Nick Hern Book

My Name Is Rachel Corrie first published in Great Britain
as a paperback original in 2005 by Nick Hern Books Limited,
14 Larden Road, London W3 7ST in association with the
Royal Court Theatre, London

Cover image: Rachel Corrie at Mima Mounds, Washington,
courtesy of the Corrie family

Typeset by Country Setting, Kingsdown, Kent CT14 8ES
Printed and bound in Great Britain by Bookmarque, Croydon,
Surrey

A CIP catalogue record for this book is available from
the British Library

ISBN 1 85459 878 3